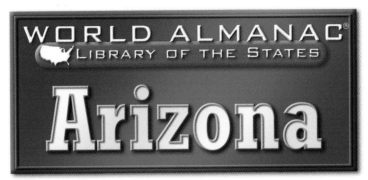

THE GRAND CANYON STATE

by Michael Martin

Curriculum Consultant: Jean Craven,
Director of Instructional Support,
Albuquerque, NM, Public Schools

WORLD ALMANAC® LIBRARY

Please visit our web site at: **www.worldalmanaclibrary.com**
For a free color catalog describing World Almanac® Library's
list of high-quality books and multimedia programs, call
1-800-848-2928 (USA) or 1-800-387-3178 (Canada).
World Almanac® Library's fax: (414) 332-3567.

Library of Congress Cataloging-in-Publication Data

Martin, Michael A.
    Arizona, the Grand Canyon State / by Michael A. Martin.
       p. cm. — (World Almanac Library of the states)
    Includes bibliographical references and index.
    Summary: Illustrations and text present the history, geography, people,
politics and government, economy, and social life and customs of Arizona,
the Grand Canyon State.
      ISBN 0-8368-5128-5 (lib. bdg.)
      ISBN 0-8368-5298-2 (softcover)
      1. Arizona—Juvenile literature. [1. Arizona.] I. Title. II. Series.
F811.3.M37   2002
979.1—dc21   2002072525

This edition first published in 2002 by
World Almanac® Library
330 West Olive Street, Suite 100
Milwaukee, WI 53212 USA

This edition © 2002 by World Almanac® Library.

Design and Editorial: Bill SMITH STUDIO Inc.
Editor: Timothy Paulson
Assistant Editor: Megan Elias
Art Director: Olga Lamm
Photo Research: Sean Livingstone
World Almanac® Library Project Editor: Patricia Lantier
World Almanac® Library Editors: Jim Mezzanotte, Monica Rausch, Lyman Lyons
World Almanac® Library Production: Tammy Gruenewald, Katherine A. Goedheer

Photo credits: pp. 4-5 © PhotoDisc; p. 6 (all) © Corel; p. 7 (top) Tucson CVB, (bottom)
© PhotoDisc; p. 9 © PhotoDisc; p. 10 © ArtToday; p. 11 © Dover; p. 12 (top) © ArtToday;
pp. 12-13 © Library of Congress; p. 14 © Bettmann/CORBIS; p. 15 © Corel; p. 17 © Library
of Congress; p. 18 © PhotoDisc; p. 19 © Kevin Fleming/CORBIS; p. 20 (left to right) © PhotoDisc,
© Corel, © Corel; p. 21 (left to right) © Corel, © PhotoDisc, © Corel; p. 23 © PhotoDisc; p. 26
(top) © PhotoDisc; pp. 26-27 © Corel; p. 29 © PhotoDisc; p. 31 © Chris Usher/TimePix; p. 33 (top)
© Corel, (inset) © Corel; p. 34 © Jeff Topping/Reuters/TimePix; p. 35 © Corel; p. 36 © Corel;
p. 37 © Corel; p. 38 © Dover; p. 39 © Dover; p. 40 © Dover; p. 41 © Arthur Schatz/TimePix;
pp. 42-43 © Library of Congress; p. 44 © PhotoDisc; p. 45 (top) © Corel, (bottom) © PhotoDisc

Printed in the United States of America

1 2 3 4 5 6 7 8 9 06 05 04 03 02

Arizona

Land of Vivid Contrasts

At first glance, Arizona may seem little more than a vast expanse of desert, yet nothing could be further from the truth. Arizona not only has deserts, mountain forests, and wildflower-strewn grasslands, but also high mesas and canyons with mighty sandstone walls that appear to prop up the sky.

Because of its dry climate, this region of the North American continent remained sparsely populated until modern times. In the mid-twentieth century, the development of large-scale irrigation systems and affordable air conditioning finally made it feasible to live there. As a result, Arizona became an increasingly popular destination for people moving west, as well as for tourists.

Arizona is home to countless wonders, both natural and artificially created. The state gets its nickname — the Grand Canyon State — from one of the great geological marvels of the world. The Grand Canyon is a giant gorge carved out of rock by Arizona's most important river, the Colorado. The canyon is 277 miles (446 kilometers) long and as much as 1 mile (1.6 km) deep. Arizona's two largest cities, Phoenix and Tucson, are human-made oases reclaimed from the desert by massive irrigation projects. The fast-growing Tucson area, in particular, is finding that it needs to strike a balance between the water needs of its population and the limited amount of usable water.

Arizona's back roads lead to many historic sites, mining towns, farm communities, and retirement villages. The Grand Canyon State also boasts twenty-six national parks and monuments, as well as a wealth of cultural treasures, including twenty-one Native American reservations. Far from being just a desert landscape, Arizona is a multidimensional place that offers something of interest to virtually everyone.

▶ Map of Arizona showing the interstate highway system, as well as major cities and waterways.

▼ The Grand Canyon offers a spectacular view of geological history.

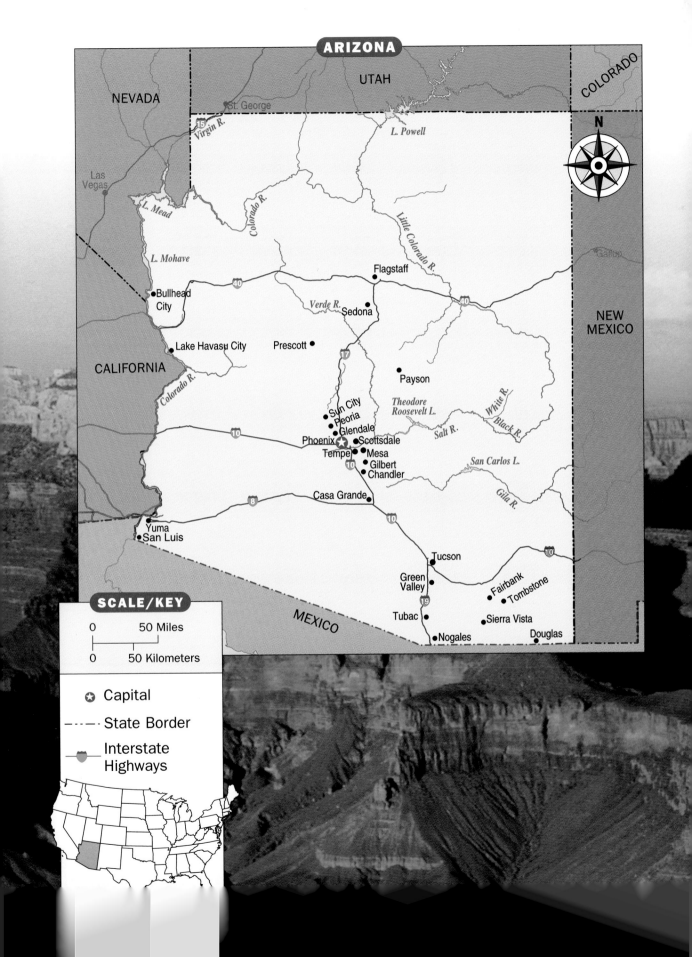

Fast Facts

ARIZONA (AZ), The Grand Canyon State

Entered Union

February 14, 1912 (48th state)

Capital	Population
Phoenix	.1,321,045

Total Population (2000)

5,130,632 (20th most populous state) — *Between 1990 and 2000, population increased by 40 percent.*

Largest Cities	Population
Phoenix	1,321,045
Tucson	486,699
Mesa	396,375
Glendale	218,812
Scottsdale	202,705

Land Area

113,635 square miles (294,315 square kilometers) (6th largest state)

State Motto

"Ditat Deus" — *Latin for "God Enriches"*

Official State Songs

"Arizona March Song," *music by Maurice Blumenthal and lyrics by Margaret Rowe Clifford, adopted in 1919;* "Arizona," *music and lyrics by Rex Allen, Jr., adopted in 1982*

State Bird

Cactus wren — *Arizona's largest wren has a peculiar song that has been compared to the sound of an automobile engine starting.*

State Tree

Paloverde

State Flower

The blossom of the saguaro cactus — *This white blossom appears on the tips of the saguaro's long arms.*

State Mammal

Ringtailed cat — *Not actually a feline, this nocturnal creature is related to the raccoon. Its bushy tail makes up about half of its length.*

State Reptile

Arizona ridge-nosed rattlesnake — *By some accounts, the Chiricahua Apaches based their war-paint designs on this creature's stripes. These rattlers are currently listed as threatened and may not be killed or captured without special permits.*

State Amphibian

Arizona tree frog

State Gemstone

Turquoise — *This blue-green, semiprecious stone has been a central element of Native American jewelry since prehistoric times.*

State Fossil

Petrified wood — *The mineralized remains of large trees that grew in Arizona more than 200 million years ago are abundant in Arizona's Petrified Forest National Park.*

PLACES TO VISIT

London Bridge, *Lake Havasu City*
This nineteenth-century stone bridge was carefully dismantled, shipped from London to Arizona, and reassembled exactly as it had been before — all 10,276 pieces of it.

Meteor Crater, *Coconino County*
This hole in the ground measures 4,180 feet (1,275 meters) wide and 570 feet (175 m) deep. It was formed 20,000 to 50,000 years ago, when a massive meteor slammed into Earth with a force so great that the meteor disintegrated into small pieces.

Tombstone, *Cochise County*
This legendary frontier settlement has been an enduring symbol of the Wild West ever since the Ike Clanton Gang traded gunfire with the Earp brothers and Doc Holliday at the O.K. Corral.

For other places and events, see p. 44.

BIGGEST, BEST, AND MOST

- Tucson has more telescopes than any other city on the planet. The world's largest solar telescope is at Kitt Peak Observatory near Tucson.

- The saguaro cactus grows only in the Sonoran Desert of the U.S. Southwest. It can reach a height of 50 feet (15 m) and live up to 200 years.

- Arizona leads the nation in copper production.

STATE FIRSTS

- **500** The ruins of Casa Grande are among the most complex prehistoric structures in North America. Built by the long-vanished Hohokam peoples, these multistory structures date back as far as A.D. 500 and include elaborate irrigation canals.

- **1915** Katherine Stinson, a Tucson stunt pilot, delivered Arizona's first "air mail."

- **1930** Clyde W. Tombaugh discovered the planet Pluto from Flagstaff's Lowell Observatory.

New Old West

Old Tucson, near Tucson, looks like a classic frontier town, but it isn't quite what it seems. Built in 1939 by Columbia Pictures for the filming of the movie *Arizona*, it is an almost full-scale copy of 1860-vintage Tucson, and it served for decades as a film and television set. Among the three hundred movies filmed there are *Gunfight at the OK Corral* (1957), *Rio Bravo* (1959), and *The Three Amigos* (1986). Although the fake town burned in a mysterious 1995 fire, it was restored and reopened within two years. It remains a significant tourist draw today, offering entertainment, living-history demonstrations, and a museum with exhibits on Native Americans and pioneer life.

Start Your Ostriches!

For decades, ostrich ranching has been an important part of commercial life in Chandler, where some city residents earn a living by selling the feathers of these birds. Ever since ostriches were introduced to the state from their native Africa, ranchers have entered them in running competitions. Chandler's chamber of commerce established its annual Ostrich Festival in 1989. Every spring, ostrich ranchers pit their best birds against one another on the racetrack.

A Thousand Gifts

Astounding land of weird and mystic scenes,
Now is the flood-tide of thy future sea,
And thousands seek a thousand gifts from thee.

*— from an anonymous poem that appeared in an
1878 edition of the* Arizona Citizen

Humans inhabited the region that is present-day Arizona perhaps as early as twelve thousand years ago. Some forty-five hundred years before Spanish explorers arrived, the land was home to Paleo-Indian hunter-gatherers known as the Cochise people — a group that vanished from the region early in the first century A.D. A millennium later, Arizona was settled by several Native American peoples, including the Anasazi, Mogollon, Patayan, and Hohokam, the last of whom are known for their extensive use of agricultural irrigation in the Santa Cruz, Salt, and Gila River valleys.

The Athapascan-speaking Apache and Navajo groups — who conquered other, mostly peaceful Native American groups in Arizona and New Mexico by the beginning of the sixteenth century — appear to have migrated to the region just before the age of European exploration. Modern-day Hopi and other pueblo groups probably are descended from the cliff-dwelling Anasazi (Navajo for "those who lived before") of the Colorado Plateau. The Pima and Papago (Tohono O'odham) have the Hohokam as their forebears.

Lure of Gold: Spanish Exploration

Inspired by tales of abundant gold and other treasures in the Arizona region, numerous Spanish expeditions headed north from Mexico in the early sixteenth century. The Franciscan priest Fray Marcos de Niza, accompanied by Estevanico, a former black slave, became the first European to survey Arizona. He passed through the San Pedro Valley in 1539 on an unsuccessful quest for treasures. Spaniard Francisco Vásquez de Coronado followed in Fray Niza's footsteps a

Native Americans of Arizona
(sixteenth century to the present)

Chiricahua Apache

Cibecue Apache

Havasupai

Hopi

Mescalero Apache

Mohave

Navajo

Pima (Akimel O'odham)

San Carlos Apache

Tohono O'odham (Papago)

Walapai

White Mountain Apache

Yavapai

Yuma

Zuñi

year later, encountering the Zuñi and Hopi. Coronado was accompanied by Don Garcia Lopez de Cardenas, who was the first European to set eyes upon the Grand Canyon. Although the stories of gold proved false, other Spanish expeditions succeeded in finding several types of mineral wealth in Arizona.

Late in the seventeenth century, Spanish Catholic priests established missions in the Arizona region, in a concerted attempt to Christianize the Native peoples. During his long clerical career, Father Eusebio Francisco Kino set up more than thirty Spanish missions in what is now northern Mexico and southern Arizona. Kino also learned a great deal about the land and its inhabitants. His explorations took him only a little further north than present-day Tombstone.

Spanish Fortifications

Many of Arizona's Native people were not happy about the Spanish presence on their land, and Native American raiders made several attempts to chase the explorers and missionaries away. The Spaniards responded by digging in

▼ One mission established by Father Eusebio Francisco Kino was San Xavier del Bac. It is located south of present-day Tucson.

Straw into Gold

In 1528, Spanish explorer Alvar Nuñez Cabeza de Vaca heard Native stories about seven wealthy cities in what is now the U.S. Southwest. He spread the story of the Seven Golden Cities of Cibola. In 1540, Francisco Vásquez de Coronado set out in search of them. He discovered a group of Zuñi cities in what is now Arizona. When the Zuñi resisted Coronado's demands for gold, his men attacked the cities and drove out the inhabitants. Coronado found no gold but continued his search. Some have speculated that the cities were called golden because the straw that was mixed with mud to create their adobe walls shone in the sun.

◀ The 1847 Battle of Chapultepec, near Mexico City, was the last major battle of the Mexican War. After losing the war, Mexico handed over the area that is now Arizona to the United States.

and building fortifications, such as the settlement at Tubac, which was established in 1752 complete with a protective fort. In 1776, the location of this presidio (garrison) was shifted to Tucson, and new fortifications, reinforced by heavy adobe walls, were erected to discourage raids against Spanish settlers.

Mexican Rule

Mexico gained its independence from Spain in 1821. Three years later, Mexico formally established the territory of New Mexico, which included Arizona. In asserting its control over the territory, the Mexican government ousted Spanish missionary teachers from schools that Spain had established in the previous century. The Mexican government suspected them of being disloyal to the new Mexican republic.

U.S. traders, in the meantime, explored the territory for furs and laid claim to parts of the Mexican lands. In 1846, the United States went to war with Mexico over territorial issues. The Mexican War was a two-year conflict that ended with the Treaty of Guadalupe Hidalgo. The treaty ceded New Mexico to the United States. Residents of northeastern states feared that the former Mexican territories would enter the United States as slave states, upsetting the balance of power in Congress between slave and free states. Congress nevertheless ratified the treaty and in 1854 authorized the Gadsden Purchase, which brought the portions of Arizona south of the Gila (pronounced *heela*) River under U.S. control. All of Arizona's non-Native settlements were confined to the region's southernmost area during this time.

Ancient Waterways

Arriving in Arizona's Salt River Valley in 1867, South Carolinian Jack Swilling was fascinated by the ruins of the ancient Hohokam civilization, especially the sophisticated irrigation system. He and his business partners restored it and made it functional, bringing water from the Salt River to the desert. By January 1, 1868, a tiny town called Pumpkinville took its place on the Arizona map. Three or four months later, Swilling and another pioneer renamed the town Phoenix, after the mythical Egyptian bird fated to die by fire and be reborn from its own ashes.

Territorial Culture Clashes

At the time of the Treaty of Guadalupe Hidalgo, most of the lands that would one day make up Arizona remained part of the New Mexico Territory, governed from the territorial capital of Santa Fe. Settlers in southern Arizona began lobbying Congress for the creation of a separate Arizona Territory during the 1850s, but without success.

When the Civil War began in 1861, many Arizona settlers from Southern states sympathized with the pro-slavery Confederacy and wanted Arizona to join it, even naming their own delegate to the Confederate Congress. In February 1862, Confederate troops seized Tucson, claiming all Arizona lands south of the 34th parallel. The U.S. Congress did not recognize the Confederacy's claim to these lands, and Union forces, led by Colonel James Carlson, quickly neutralized the Confederate military presence in Arizona.

Prompted by Confederate interest in the Union's southwestern territories, the U.S. Congress acted in 1863 to establish a separate Arizona Territory, with approximately the same borders as the present-day state. On December 27 of that year, John N. Goodwin was installed at Fort Whipple as the region's first territorial governor. Goodwin's log house, located a short distance from the fort, later became the nucleus of the town of Prescott.

Non-Native settlers began moving into areas inhabited or used by Native Americans. At first, most Native people were willing to share land, and treaties were made between the two groups. It quickly became clear, however, that white settlers wanted to own and control land, rather than share it, and many did not respect Native cultures and customs. The U.S. government often broke treaties with Native people in Arizona when it served the interests of white settlers.

Native leaders, such as Cochise and Geronimo, both Apache, encouraged their people

Navajo War

In 1858, Manuelito, a Navajo leader, discovered that many of his cattle had been shot by U.S. soldiers. When he complained, soldiers burned his village and farm. Joined by Barboncito, a Navajo medicine man and war chief, Manuelito led forces against the U.S. Army at Fort Defiance. The U.S. Army responded by declaring total war on the Navajo. From 1863 to 1864, Kit Carson *(above)*, who had won fame as a trader and scout in the region and was now a colonel in the Union Army, attacked the Navajo and burned their fields. By 1864, he had rounded up some eight thousand Navajo people and moved them forcibly to a reservation in New Mexico. Many died along the way, and others died on the reservation, where conditions were harsh. In 1868, Barboncito negotiated with General William T. Sherman, who was Commander in Chief of U.S. forces in the West. Sherman wanted to relocate the Navajo to Oklahoma, but Barboncito got him to agree to let them return home. The reservation established for the Navajo on the Arizona-New Mexico border was once small, but it has since grown into the largest Native reservation in the United States.

to resist white settlement of their ancestral territories. Cochise began leading raids against U.S. army posts in 1862, after several of his family members were killed by U.S. soldiers for a crime they did not commit. Cochise and his band of warriors fought against the U.S. Army for nearly ten years, hiding out in the mountains and conducting raids on white settlements and army posts. Cochise surrendered in 1872 and went to live with his people on the Chiricahua Reservation in southeastern Arizona.

▲ Geronimo and his men negotiate with U.S. general George Crook.

When the U.S. government relocated the Chiricahua residents to a barren reservation in New Mexico, a group of Apache, led by Geronimo, fought to escape this virtual imprisonment. In 1885, Geronimo and his warriors fought the U.S. Army for almost a year in an attempt to stay off the reservation. He was captured by General George Crook but escaped two days later. The next year, Geronimo surrendered to General Nelson Miles and was sent with some of his supporters to Florida, Alabama, and eventually Fort Sills, Oklahoma. They had been promised that their families could go with them, but the government did not allow this to happen. Geronimo never saw Arizona again.

During the 1860s and 1870s, the Arizona Territory made considerable strides in agriculture, natural resource development, and transportation. Farms in the Salt River Valley, near Phoenix, began practicing modern irrigation during the late 1860s. The next decade saw the establishment of sheep- and cattle-ranching operations. The Southern Pacific Railroad linked Arizona and California on September 30, 1877. During the next decade, the Southern Pacific and Santa Fe Railroads were built across southern and northern Arizona, respectively. The discovery of gold

▼ The Theodore Roosevelt Dam, built in 1911, helps supply the state with water for agriculture and hydroelectric power.

and silver in 1877, near what would become Tombstone, brought an influx of miners. Copper mining also flourished.

Statehood

Arizona formally achieved statehood on February 14, 1912, becoming the last of the contiguous forty-eight states to enter the Union. The course of the state's early history was greatly influenced by its first governor, George W. P. Hunt. During his fourteen years of service, Hunt, a Democrat, led a movement to build dams and irrigation systems, and he helped attract federal programs designed to bring much-needed water to the state's rapidly growing farms, towns, and cities. The ranching, mining, and tourism industries also prospered under Hunt's leadership.

The Theodore Roosevelt Dam, located on the Salt River east of Phoenix, was completed in 1911 and was Arizona's first large-scale source of irrigation water in the twentieth century. The next quarter-century saw a huge increase in the state's arable lands — and in its agricultural production — thanks to the completion of several other important dams. These included three other Salt River dams, as well as the Gila River's Coolidge Dam, the Verde River's Bartlett Dam, and the Colorado River's Hoover Dam. Completed in 1936, the Hoover Dam is the state's largest.

Boom, Bust, and Boom

The outbreak of World War I, in 1914, spurred tremendous increases in the production of both cotton and copper in Arizona. The Goodyear Company established the town of Goodyear, where vast quantities of cotton fiber were produced for use in the manufacture of tires and other war-related rubber products. Arizona's copper was processed for ammunition, and the state's burgeoning cattle-ranching industry provided food for thousands of U.S. soldiers.

Arizona in World War I

When the United States entered World War I, Arizonans lined up to fight for their country. The first Arizonan known to have died in battle was Matthew Juan, a Pima (Akimel O'odham) Indian from Sacaton. Two Arizonans received the Congressional Medal of Honor for their valor. John Henry Pruitt, a U.S. Marine from Camp Verde, was decorated posthumously for his single-handed capture of forty German soldiers. Lieutenant Frank Luke, Jr., of Phoenix, shot down fourteen German observation balloons and four planes in just seventeen days. His airplane was forced down, and he was killed in a shoot-out with German troops. The Germans were so impressed by Lieutenant Luke's bravery that they gave him a hero's burial.

Following the end of World War I, in 1918, Arizona's mining industry suffered when the copper market collapsed. The state was jolted again by the Great Depression, which began in 1929 and lasted through the 1930s, causing mass unemployment across the country. Many of the nation's dislocated workers, including thousands of people fleeing the drought conditions in Oklahoma and other Dust Bowl states, sought new livelihoods in California. A number of these migrants stopped in Arizona along the way and decided to remain permanently in or near Phoenix and Tucson. During the 1920s and 1930s, Arizona's population swelled from about 340,000 to nearly half a million.

▲ Raul Castro, Arizona governor from 1975 to 1977. In 1977, Castro became U.S. Ambassador to Argentina.

World War II and the Postwar Years

The entry of the United States into World War II in 1941 brought new jobs and more residents to the state. The U.S. government selected Arizona — whose warm, dry climate provided superb year-round flying conditions — as the site for several Air Force bases. War production boosted Arizona's output of cattle, copper, and cotton. The state experienced a population explosion as thousands of workers and, later, World War II veterans discovered the advantages of life in the Southwest. Thanks to the easy availability of water and air-conditioning systems, Arizona's once-forbidding desert climate also became attractive to many retirees. In the 1940s, for example, Arizona's population rose by about 50 percent. The 1950s brought an even bigger increase. During the 1950s and 1960s, Arizona's economy shifted from agriculture toward manufacturing. The number of tourists to the state also increased.

Political Progress and Upheaval

Arizona's Native Americans finally gained the right to vote in 1948, after the Arizona Supreme Court overturned prohibitions written into the state constitution. In 1965, Judge Lorna Lockwood broke an important gender barrier when her fellow judges elected her as chief justice of the Arizona Supreme Court, making her the first woman in U.S. history to head a state supreme court. Democrat Raul H. Castro became Arizona's first Mexican-American governor

The Navajo Code

A critical factor in the Allied victory over Japan in World War II was the ability of U.S. combat units to exchange secure messages. At first, Japanese code breakers were cracking almost any code the U.S. military could develop. The U.S. government sought help from the Navajo, whose language is considered extremely difficult. Navajo Marines created and memorized an incredibly complex code based on Navajo words. About four hundred Navajo speakers were attached to U.S. Marine units in the Pacific, to send and receive messages. Not only were the Japanese unable to break the code, they didn't even know how to write it down.

in 1975. In 1981, President Ronald Reagan named Arizonan Sandra Day O'Connor to the U.S. Supreme Court, giving the nation's highest court its first female justice.

Blooms in the Desert

The water supply has continued to affect the state's history through the end of the twentieth century and into the twenty-first. By the 1960s, Arizona had begun to deplete its water resources. The natural underground water supplies were drying up. To address this problem, Arizona engaged in a lengthy legal battle with California over water rights to the Colorado and Gila Rivers. In a ruling in 1963, the U.S. Supreme Court granted Arizona annual access to the entire flow of the Gila River and a portion of the Colorado River. This amount was deemed enough to sustain about fourteen million urban dwellers. In 1974, in an effort to ensure Arizona's future water supply, the state began constructing a system of water pipelines and aqueducts known as the Central Arizona Project. Completed in 1991, these conduits run from Lake Havasu on the Colorado River to the San Xavier Indian Reservation, southwest of Tucson.

Throughout this period, Arizona's increasingly urban population continued to grow. As the twenty-first century began, this growth rate appeared to have leveled off somewhat, but Arizona's clear skies and relaxed lifestyle are still irresistible to many.

▼ The Central Arizona Project aqueduct, with Picacho Peak in the distance.

Dwellers in Wide-Open Spaces

The people of the frontier, while they should as far as possible feel contented with their lot, have much to look forward to and much to hope for, and they have a great responsibility in shaping the destinies of the future State.

— *Judge William J. Berry, editor of the* Yuma Sentinel, *circa 1875*

Arizona is the sixth-largest state in the United States, but its population is relatively small — 5,130,632, according to the 2000 Census. This ranks Arizona twentieth among the fifty states. In terms of population growth rate, however, Arizona is a pacesetter. Between 1990 and 2000, the state's population increased by 40 percent — more than triple the national average (13.1 percent). There are several reasons for this impressive rate. First, the state has enjoyed a steady stream of people relocating to Arizona. Second, since the state's population is relatively small, a thousand new residents will boost its overall population by a higher percentage than would a thousand new residents in a more populous state. A third reason is that births in Arizona exceed deaths by more than two to one.

Age Distribution in Arizona
(2000 Census)

0–4	382,386
5–19	1,135,802
20–24	362,860
25–44	1,511,469
45–64	1,070,276
65 & over	667,839

Across the Decades

Arizona's three largest foreign-born groups for 1920 and 1990

■ 1920   ■ 1990

Mexico	England	Canada
60,325	2,882	1,962

Total state population: 334,162
Total foreign-born: 78,099 (23%)

Mexico	Canada	Germany
150,068	16,451	11,548

Total state population: 3,665,228
Total foreign-born: 278,205 (8%)

Patterns of Immigration

The total number of people who immigrated to Arizona in 1999 was 2,376. Of that number, the largest immigrant groups were from Mexico (33%), India (8%), and China (4.5%).

Where Do Arizonans Live?

More than 80 percent of Arizona's residents live in towns and cities, and some three-quarters of these people call the Phoenix-Mesa area home. Phoenix is Arizona's capital and largest city. Many other Arizonans live in and around the city of Tucson. Both of these cities have experienced spurts of rapid growth since the early part of the twentieth century. Large communities of retirees, such as those in Sun City (near Phoenix) and Green Valley (near Tucson), have sprung up over the past fifty years as well.

A Dash of Diversity

The military defeats suffered by the Apache and Navajo during the 1860s provided the initial stimulus for new settlement in Arizona, mostly by English-speaking people from Texas and other Southern states. Spanish-speaking Mexican people, already a strong presence in the region

▲ Students at the teacher training school in Tempe in 1908.

Heritage and Background, Arizona   Year 2000

▶ Here's a look at the racial backgrounds of Arizonans today. Arizona ranks thirty-fifth among all U.S. states with regard to African Americans as a percentage of the population.

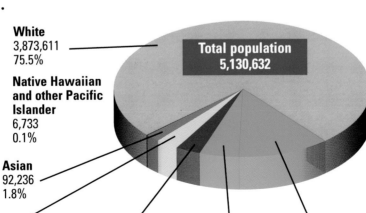

White
3,873,611
75.5%

Native Hawaiian and other Pacific Islander
6,733
0.1%

Asian
92,236
1.8%

Total population
5,130,632

Two or more races
146,526
2.9%

Black or African American
158,873
3.1%

American Indian and Alaska Native
255,879
5.0%

Some other race
596,774
11.6%

Note: 25.3% (1,295,617) of the population identify themselves as **Hispanic** or **Latino,** a cultural designation that crosses racial lines. Hispanics and Latinos are counted in this category as well as the racial category of their choice.

because of Arizona's historic ties to Mexico and Spain, referred to these newcomers as Anglos.

The rapid development of Arizona's cotton, copper-mining, and cattle-ranching industries encouraged further population growth. Miners from Mexico and European countries such as Ireland, Scotland, England, Germany, Italy, and Serbia, as well as from Russia, arrived in ever-greater numbers during the copper-boom years of the late nineteenth and early twentieth centuries. Mexican immigration to Arizona remains strong today.

More than three-fourths of Arizona's present population is of European ancestry, many descended from the region's original white settlers. Slightly more than a quarter of the population is Hispanic, a group that overlaps with Arizona's self-described "white" population, because many people see themselves as falling into multiple categories. The population's Mexican heritage is evident in everything from place names to festivals and holidays. Native Americans, primarily Hopi and Navajo, make up 5 percent of the state's population, while 3.1 percent are of African descent. Only 1.8 percent of Arizonans are of Asian descent.

Arizona's median age is 34.2, slightly younger than the national average (35.3). Females edge out males,

▼ Phoenix is the sixth-largest city in the United States. Greater Phoenix covers 2,000 square miles (5,180 square km). Between 1920 and 2000, the city's population rose from a little over twenty-nine thousand to more than one million.

representing 50.1 percent of the state's population.

Education

Arizona's first public school was established in Tucson in 1871. Today, Arizona law requires children to attend school from ages six through fifteen; the education of those who live on reservations is overseen by the Federal Bureau of Indian Affairs.

The University of Arizona, established in Tucson in 1885 by the territorial legislature, was the territory's first institution of higher learning. Tempe's Arizona Territorial Normal School, established in 1885 as a teacher training college, later became Arizona State University.

Religion

Arizona's Spanish settlers brought Roman Catholicism with them. After the territory became a state, Protestant faiths predominated among Arizona's Anglo population, while its Hispanic population remained mostly Catholic. Today, 79.5 percent of Arizonans identify themselves as Christians. Catholics make up about 20 percent of the population. Among Protestant denominations are Baptists, who make up 11 percent of the population; Methodists, who make up nearly 7 percent of the population; and Lutherans, who make up about 5 percent. Some 5.6 percent practice Native American religions, while Jews and Buddhists each represent about 1 percent of the population. Two-tenths of 1 percent of the state's residents are Muslim.

▲ Navajo students play basketball at Fort Defiance School on the Navajo Indian Reservation. The Fort Defiance Agency manages social services in an area of the Navajo Nation.

Educational Levels of Arizona Workers (age 25 and over)	
Less than 9th grade	207,509
9th to 12th grade, no diploma	283,571
High school graduate, including equivalency	601,440
Some college, no degree or associate degree	741,784
Bachelor's degree	306,554
Graduate or professional degree	160,319

New World, Ancient Wonders

I love you, Arizona;
Your mountains, deserts, and streams;
The rise of Dos Cabezas
And the outlaws I see in my dreams. . . .
I love you, Arizona;
Desert dust on the wind;
The sage and cactus are blooming,
And the smell of the rain on your skin.

— "Arizona," music and lyrics by Rex Allen, Jr., 1981

The portions of the Colorado Plateau that extend into Arizona reach altitudes of 5,000 to 12,633 feet (1,524 to 3,851 m). Where these extensions are relatively level, they are marked by basins, natural stone arches, igneous domes, and volcanic fields. The plateau's most prominent feature is the Grand Canyon, a mile-deep chasm that was carved out of rock over eons by the Colorado River. All of the region's other rivers and streams drain into the Colorado. Some of these tributaries have carved canyons, such as Oak Creek Canyon and Canyon de Chelly. The Colorado Plateau's highest point, Humphreys Peak, is also the highest point in the state.

Climate

Although Arizona tends to be warm, sunny, and dry, the state's climate varies considerably depending on

Highest Point

Humphreys Peak
12,633 feet (3,851 m)
above sea level

▼ *From left to right:* Meteor Crater; a bobcat; conifers in the White Mountains; the Colorado River; the Mittens of Monument Valley; a sidewinder rattlesnake.

topography and elevation. This area of the Southwest is generally hot and arid, but in the higher elevations, winters are frigid and snowy, with temperatures colder than 0° Fahrenheit (–18° Celsius). Desert areas seldom reach freezing. Annual precipitation also varies by region. Arizona's southwestern deserts receive only about 2 to 5 inches (5 to 13 cm) annually, while the mountainous regions can get more than 30 inches (76 cm).

The Land and Its Resources

Arizona's southern regions have yielded an abundance of useful minerals. Gold and silver were discovered in Arizona in 1877. The state is also rich in coal, which has been found principally on the Navajo Indian Reservation and is still mined today. Other Arizona mines supply lead, molybdenum, uranium, zinc, and sand and gravel. Because about a third of Arizona's land area supports forests, a healthy lumber industry exists in the state. Arizona's cities and farms depend greatly on subsurface water supplies, or aquifers. This began to change in 1991, when the Central Arizona Project aqueduct brought water from the Colorado River to Phoenix, Tucson, and various farming regions in the state.

A River Runs Through It

Arizona's largest waterway and water source is the Colorado River, which defines most of the state's western border. The river enters Arizona from Utah, near the center of the northern border, then winds west through the Grand Canyon before turning south. Lake Mead, which forms part of the Arizona-Nevada border, is a reservoir on the Colorado River, providing recreation, fishing, and hydroelectric power. Arizona is also home to a large number of arroyos (dry riverbeds), which contain subsurface streams and occasionally flood on the surface.

Average January temperature
Flagstaff: 30°F (-1°C)
Tucson: 52°F (11°C)

Average July temperature
Flagstaff: 66°F (19°C)
Tucson: 87°F (31°C)

Average yearly rainfall
Flagstaff: 22.8 inches (57.9 cm)
Tucson: 12.0 inches (30.5 cm)

Average yearly snowfall
Flagstaff: 108.8 inches (276.4 cm)
Tucson: 0.0 inches (0.0 cm)

Major Rivers

Colorado River
1,450 miles (2,333 km)

Gila River
649 miles (1,044 km)

Little Colorado River
300 miles (483 km)

DID YOU KNOW?

The most extensive Ponderosa pine forests on Earth are located in Arizona's mountainous Mogollon Plateau region.

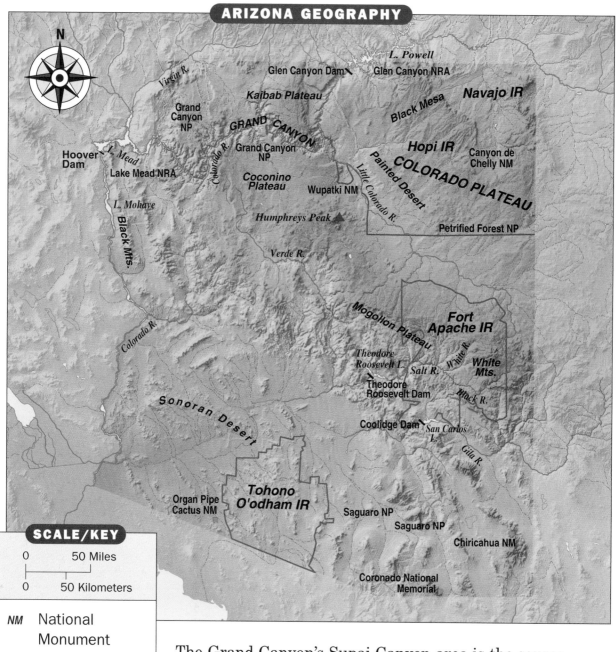

SCALE/KEY

0	50 Miles
0	50 Kilometers

NM	National Monument
NP	National Park
NRA	National Recreation Area
IR	Indian Reservation
▲	Highest Point
	Mountains

The Grand Canyon's Supai Canyon area is the source of several spectacular waterfalls.

Arizona's natural lakes are generally small and confined to mountainous regions. The state's larger lakes were created mainly by building dams on the Colorado River. Among them are Hoover Dam (which created Lake Mead), Glen Canyon Dam (Lake Powell), and Parker Dam (Lake Havasu). The Gila and Salt Rivers are known for the Coolidge and Theodore Roosevelt Dams, respectively, while Horseshoe Dam and Bartlett Dam are located on the Verde River.

Plants and Wildlife

Some 42 percent of Arizona's land area supports the type of vegetation found in the Sonoran Desert, such as the creosote bush and sage (or burro bush). The plant most identified with this southern upland desert is the giant saguaro cactus, characterized by its many branches. It is the nation's largest cactus. The organ-pipe cactus can be found in desert zones closer to sea level. Other plants in the upland desert are mesquite; ocotillo; paloverde; and barrel, cholla, and prickly pear cacti. Arizona's wildflowers include the golden columbine, paintbrush, phlox, pink, poppy, and sand verbena. Arizona's high-elevation forests abound with ponderosa pine, aspen, Douglas and white firs, cottonwood, and walnut. At lower elevations, juniper, piñon, manzanita, and sumac blend into chaparral and mesquite-rich grassland zones.

Arizona's mountain forests provide a habitat for bear, bighorn sheep, elk, bobcats, and mountain lions. The deserts and grasslands support pronghorn antelope, coyotes, javelinas (wild pigs), and rabbits, as well as reptiles such as king snakes, rattlesnakes, rosy boas, and more than forty types of lizards, including the rarely seen, poisonous Gila monster. Coral snakes, as well as tarantulas and scorpions, thrive in the desert. Badgers, beavers, foxes, raccoons, skunks, and weasels also live in Arizona. The fish in the state's rivers and lakes include bluegill, catfish, bass, and trout. The broad-tailed hummingbird, cactus wren, and red-tailed hawk can be seen in Arizona's many bird-watching destinations, such as Madera Canyon.

Largest Lakes
Lake Powell 170,240 acres (68,896 ha)
Lake Mead 158,080 acres (63,975 ha)
Lake Mohave 28,160 acres (11,396 ha)

▼ Organ Pipe Cactus National Monument in the Sonoran Desert.

Riches in a Rugged Land

> The kind of informal, outdoor, neighborly, spacious life which brings so many people to our state would be an inevitable casualty of unlimited growth.
>
> — *Morris K. Udall, "Spaceship Earth: Standing Room Only — A Bold Plan to Save Us From Ourselves,"* Arizona Magazine, *July 27, 1969*

Arizona's natural variety is mirrored by its economic diversity. Agriculture, manufacturing, mining, and tourism all contribute to the health and stability of the state's dynamic economy.

The 1870s brought the railroads to the Arizona Territory. Driven by mining activity, Arizona continued building a transportation network, through the early days of statehood and beyond. Modern Arizona's freight and passenger transportation needs are served by rail, airports, interstate highways, state highways, and even Native American trails. Approximately 54,000 miles (87,000 km) of roads and highways now crisscross the state. Thanks to Arizona's comprehensive transportation network, even remote parts of the state are now accessible with relative ease.

Buried Treasure

In 1900, the copper-mining town of Bisbee was the busiest and most populous place in Arizona. That has since changed, but Arizona remains the nation's leading copper producer, accounting for about 60 percent of the nation's annual production. Turquoise, gold, silver, coal, petroleum, uranium, lime, pumice, crushed stone, sand, and gravel are also important products extracted from Arizona's earth. The steel-hardening agents vanadium and molybdenum are also mined in the state.

Top Employers
(of workers age sixteen and over)

Services	34.6%
Wholesale and retail trade	22.3%
Manufacturing	12.9%
Finance, insurance, and real estate	7.5%
Transportation, communications, and other public utilities	7.3%
Construction	6.7%
Public Administration	5.4%
Agriculture, forestry, and fisheries	2.5%
Mining	0.9%

ARIZONA ECONOMY

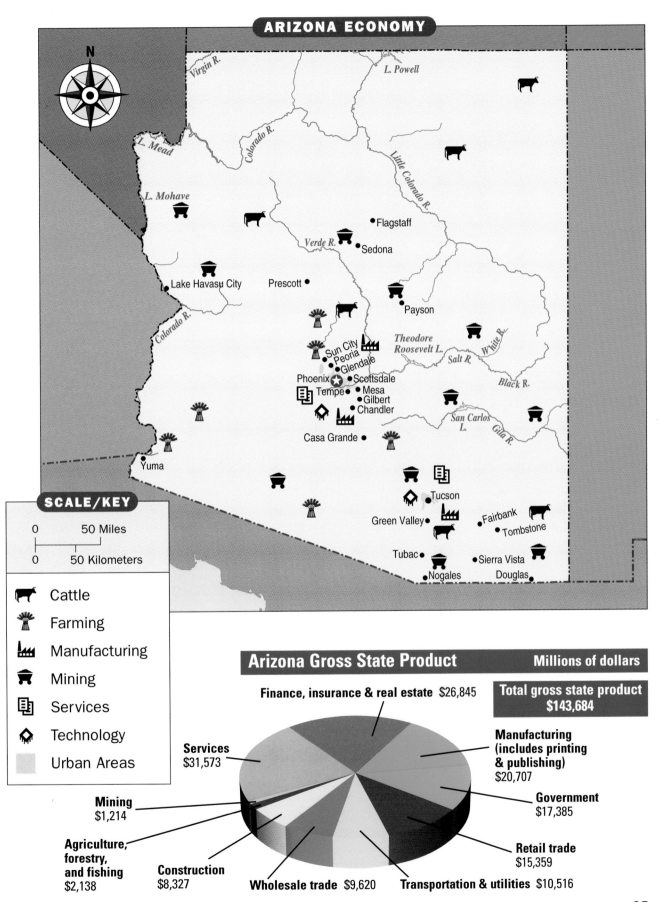

SCALE/KEY

0 — 50 Miles
0 — 50 Kilometers

- 🐂 Cattle
- 🌾 Farming
- 🏭 Manufacturing
- ⛏ Mining
- 📑 Services
- ◈ Technology
- ▨ Urban Areas

Arizona Gross State Product — Millions of dollars

Total gross state product $143,684

- Finance, insurance & real estate $26,845
- Services $31,573
- Manufacturing (includes printing & publishing) $20,707
- Government $17,385
- Mining $1,214
- Retail trade $15,359
- Agriculture, forestry, and fishing $2,138
- Construction $8,327
- Wholesale trade $9,620
- Transportation & utilities $10,516

Desert Cultivation

Arizona is home to about 7,400 farms and ranches, covering approximately half the state's land. About 95 percent of this land, especially in northern and southeastern Arizona, is used for grazing cattle and sheep. Despite the fact that cattle raising is the state's single largest source of farm income, sales of livestock and livestock products account for less than half of Arizona's annual farm revenues. Cotton is Arizona's most important crop, and has been since the territorial period. Alfalfa, raised mainly as cattle feed, and grains, such as wheat, corn, sorghum, and barley, are also widely cultivated. Yuma and Maricopa Counties excel in both vegetable and citrus fruit production, while Pinal and Pima Counties are known for pecans. Arizona is one of the nation's leaders in lettuce farming.

Manufacturing

During the 1950s and 1960s, Arizona's economy moved away from agriculture toward manufacturing. The Phoenix metropolitan area is the state's industrial leader. Motorola, a giant in telecommunications and electronics, is the city's — and Arizona's — largest employer. The state's second-largest employer is the Tucson-based Hughes Aircraft Company. Semiconductors for computers are manufactured in plants located in Chandler, Mesa, Phoenix, and Tempe. Tempe factories also make machine parts. Factories in the Phoenix area manufacture radios, turbine engines, and even spacecraft. Scottsdale produces electronic communication systems. Tucson is a source for transportation equipment and guided missiles, while factories in Mesa make helicopters.

Made in Arizona

Leading farm products and crops
Beef cattle
Cotton
Sheep
Lettuce
Citrus fruit
Wheat
Grains
Alfalfa
Vegetables

Other products
Electronic equipment
Transportation equipment
Communication systems
Aircraft
Apparel
Scientific instruments

Service Industries

Since the 1980s, the state's service industries have emerged as the major contributor to Arizona's gross state product — that is, the total annual value of the state's goods and services. Most of Arizona's service industries are based in its two largest population centers, Phoenix and Tucson. Community, business, and personal services account for the largest share of the gross state product, employing more people than any other type of economic activity. These businesses include law firms, private health-care providers, repair shops, and hotels. Other service sectors are finance, insurance, and real estate; wholesale and retail businesses; transportation; communications; utilities; and government services, including public schools, state universities, and public hospitals, as well as services found on Native American reservations and military bases.

Major Airports		
Airport	Location	Passengers per year (2000)
Phoenix Sky Harbor International	Phoenix	36,040,469
Tucson International	Tucson	3,592,188
Yuma International	Yuma	115,904

Tourism

From November through April, millions travel to Arizona in search of warm, dry weather. These visitors not only bring money into the state, they also temporarily double the population in certain cities.

While labor strife and declining copper prices have adversely affected Arizona's mining industry in recent decades, the state's perennial appeal as a tourist destination keeps the state's economy vibrant. Industrial diversification adds to this bright economic outlook.

▼ Massive irrigation projects make it possible to grow crops, such as lettuce, in the arid terrain of Arizona.

An Independent Tradition

> A frequent recurrence to fundamental principles is essential to the security of individual rights and the perpetuity of free government.
>
> — *Arizona State Constitution, Declaration of Rights, Section 1, 1911*

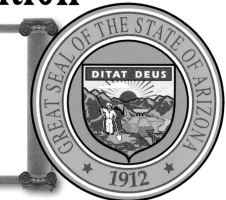

Residents of territorial Arizona began agitating for statehood in the 1890s, but the U.S. Congress did not allow Arizona to make a formal application until 1910. Even then, a crucial roadblock remained — President William Howard Taft vetoed the congressional bill granting Arizona statehood because the territory's newly drafted constitution, adopted February 9, 1911, allowed voters the option of removing judges from office by a popular vote. This clause was removed, and Arizona entered the Union on February 14, 1912, becoming the forty-eighth state. Shortly thereafter, Arizona amended its constitution yet again — this time to restore the people's right to remove judges. The city of Phoenix, which had been the territorial capital since 1889, became Arizona's permanent state capital.

State Constitution

All political power is inherent in the people, and governments derive their just powers from the consent of the governed, and are established to protect and maintain individual rights.

— *Article II, Declaration of Rights, Section 2 in the Arizona Constitution, 1911*

Executive Branch

Arizona's chief executive officer is the governor. The governor is elected to a four-year term. There is no limit to the total number of terms a governor may serve, but no governor may serve more than two consecutive terms. (The same rule applies to the offices of the secretary of state, attorney general, state treasurer, and superintendent of public instruction.) The governor's duties include proposing legislation and budgeting in support of legislation. The governor may also veto legislation, preventing it from being passed into law unless a two-thirds majority (three-quarters for an emergency bill) of the state house and senate override the veto. The governor appoints the heads of several governmental agencies and represents the state at national and international events. Because the office of lieutenant governor does not exist in Arizona, the secretary of state is the legal successor if the governor dies, is removed from office, or resigns. Next in the line of succession are, in order, the attorney general, state treasurer, and superintendent of public instruction.

Legislative Branch

Arizona's bicameral (two-housed) legislature is made up of a sixty-member house of representatives and a thirty-member senate. Voters in each legislative district (there are thirty in all) elect two representatives and one senator. Term-limit laws, instituted in 2000, stipulate that these officials may serve no more than four two-year terms. The legislature officially starts its session on the second Monday of each January, and it is required to adjourn by the Saturday following the hundredth day. The speaker of the house and the president of the senate may convene an

Elected Posts in the Executive Branch		
Office	**Length of Term**	**Term Limits**
Governor	4 years	2 consecutive terms
Secretary of State	4 years	2 consecutive terms
Attorney General	4 years	2 consecutive terms
State Treasurer	4 years	2 consecutive terms
Superintendent of Public Instruction	4 years	2 consecutive terms

Do Over!

In Arizona's 1916 election, voters were allowed to check a box on their ballots to indicate that they wished to vote for all the candidates of either the Democratic or Republican party. A majority selected the Democratic ticket, but many of them also marked the box for the Republican gubernatorial candidate. When the votes were counted, Democratic governor George W. P. Hunt apparently lost to his Republican challenger, Thomas E. Campbell, by thirty votes. Hunt disputed the mismarked ballots. Both men took the oath of office while the final outcome was being determined. After a superior court decided in Campbell's favor, Hunt took the matter to the Arizona Supreme Court. On December 22, 1917, the high court overturned the lower court's decision, giving the election to Hunt.

▼ The Arizona State Capitol, completed in 1900.

overtime session for a period of no more than seven days. Only a majority vote of both legislative houses, or a call by the governor for a special legislative session of indefinite length, can extend the time limit. Members of the legislature propose bills, discuss them in committees and larger sessions, and vote on them as a group. Legislation approved in the house is then sent to the senate for discussion and a vote. If both houses approve a bill, it is sent to the governor, who reviews it and either signs it into law or vetoes it.

Arizona citizens may also propose legislation through an initiative or a referendum. An initiative is a proposal that an issue should be put before the voters of the state. An initiative may be proposed by 10 percent of the voters. A referendum is a proposal to submit a measure already passed by the legislature to a popular vote. A referendum may be proposed either by the legislature or by 5 percent of the voters. An initiative or a referendum will become law if approved by a majority of voters. In order to pass an amendment to the constitution, at least 15 percent of Arizona voters must approve the amendment.

Arizona voters also have the right to recall any elected official, including judges, if they are dissatisfied with the way an official is performing his or her duties. Recall operates through the referendum process.

Judicial Branch

Arizona's highest court is called the supreme court. It consists of five justices, who are appointed by the governor to six-year terms. The governor selects them from a list furnished by a commission on appellate court appointments. After a justice serves his or her term, Arizona's voters cast ballots to determine whether or not the judge should remain on the court. The chief justice is selected by a vote of the justices and serves a five-year term.

Arizona's court of appeals, established in 1965, has divisions based in Phoenix and Tucson, consisting of fifteen

State Legislature			
House	**Number of Members**	**Length of Term**	**Term Limits**
Senate	30 senators	2 years	4 terms
House of Representatives	60 representatives	2 years	4 terms

and six judges, respectively. These judges also serve six-year terms, and their selection and retention is handled in the same manner as the state supreme court justices. Each county has its own superior court, where most of the important civil and criminal cases are heard. In most counties, voters elect superior court judges to four-year terms.

Party Politics

Arizonans tended to vote for Democrats until the 1952 election to the U.S. Senate of conservative Republican Barry Goldwater. Goldwater went on to make a bid for the U.S. presidency in 1964, only to be defeated by incumbent president Lyndon B. Johnson, a Texas Democrat.

The Republican party tends to dominate in Phoenix and Tucson, while Democrats are strong in Arizona's smaller towns and rural areas. Since achieving statehood, Arizona has awarded its electoral votes to Republican presidential candidates in approximately two out of every three elections.

Dine Bikeyah

The Navajo Nation, which is one of the largest Native American nations in the United States, has approximately 250,000 members. As an Indian nation, the Navajo have a unique legal relationship with the United States. The Nation is considered sovereign, but has limits on its authority. The geographic area of the Nation, known as Dine Bikeyah, extends through parts of Arizona, Utah, and New Mexico. Tribal government has its headquarters in Window Rock, Arizona, and consists of executive, legislative, and judicial branches. The nation is governed by a council with eighty-eight members, who are elected by Navajo voters. The Nation also elects a president and vice president, who preside over governmental divisions and offices that provide social services. The Speaker of the Navajo Nation presides over the legislative branch, which consists of boards and offices. The judicial branch includes a supreme court, seven district courts, and a number of family courts.

The "Straight Talk" Express

No Arizonan has ever served as president of the United States, but John McCain, a U.S. senator from Arizona, made an attempt to win the 2000 Republican presidential nomination. McCain (born in 1936) was a Navy aviator for twenty-two years. During the Vietnam War, his aircraft was shot down, and McCain survived more than five years of imprisonment and torture in Hanoi. In 1982, he was elected to serve Arizona in the U.S. House of Representatives. He spent two terms there before being elected to the U.S. Senate. Throughout his long political career, McCain has crusaded against wasteful government spending and the influence of corporations and special-interest groups.

Sing of the Great Southwest

> Sing the song that's in your hearts
> Sing of the great Southwest,
> Thank God, for Arizona
> In splendid sunshine dressed.
> For thy beauty and thy grandeur,
> For thy regal robes so sheen
> We hail thee Arizona
> Our Goddess and our queen.
>
> *— Arizona's state anthem, "Arizona March Song," music by Maurice Blumenthal, lyrics by Margaret Rowe Clifford, 1915*

Arizona's Grand Canyon is one of the most popular tourist destinations in the world. There are many ways to enjoy the canyon, from mule-back rides on its steep paths to helicopter rides to white-water rafting down the Colorado River, which runs through the middle of the canyon. Some prefer simply to drive along the rim and watch the sun as it sets over the glorious scenery.

Among other natural wonders found in the state are the Petrified Forest and the Painted Desert. Petrified Forest National Park is a 93,533-acre (37,853-ha) expanse of desert wilderness, in which can be found the world's largest concentration of petrified wood. Petrified wood is the result of silica coating decaying trees over thousands of years. What was once a great forest is now a splendid array of richly colored stones, lying on the desert floor.

The Painted Desert features a group of eroded hills that are colored in remarkably bright hues. They are composed of a combination of hematite, which is a red stone; limonite, which is yellow; and gypsum, which is white. The stones have been ground down over many centuries by water and wind.

Breathtaking scenery also can be found in Monument Valley Navajo Tribal Park and in Canyon de Chelly National Monument, where stone mesas, buttes, and spires have been shaped by erosion into strange figures. Mesas

Grand Canyon Folklore

Long before scientists unlocked the geological secrets of the Grand Canyon, Arizona's Native peoples had come up with explanations of their own. According to the Walapai people, a great flood engulfed the entire world long ago, drowning all of its inhabitants except for a giant creature called Pack-i-tha-wi. Pack-i-tha-wi waded into the flood-waters and used a wooden club to drive his flint knife into the submerged earth, thus draining away the water and creating the Grand Canyon. When the desert sun rose the next day, it baked the canyon into its current dry, cracked form.

and buttes are small hills with flat tops and often steep sides that have been formed by the erosion of land around them. Some of the most spectacular formations are the Mittens — huge, mitt-shaped rocks — in Monument Valley, and the Spider Rocks in Canyon de Chelly, which rise like narrow towers from the desert floor.

The Lively Arts

Classical music is an integral part of the Arizona arts scene. The state capital is home to the world-class Phoenix Symphony, which performs at the Arizona State Auditorium, as does the Arizona Opera. Other cities, such as Mesa and Scottsdale, also have professional symphony orchestras. The boys choirs of Phoenix and Tucson have enthusiastic followings, as do the Orpheus Men's Chorus and the Phabulous Phoenicians barbershop singers (both from Phoenix). The Sedona Jazz on the Rocks festival, held each September, features many famous musical ensembles that draw jazz fans from all over.

Arts and Crafts

The art forms most commonly associated with Arizona and the American Southwest are those of Native American people. The handcrafted rugs and sandpaintings of the Navajo are admired throughout the world. The Papago (Tohono O'odham) are renowned for their intricately woven baskets, and pottery-making is a time-honored tradition across the Southwest. Multitalented artist R. C. Gorman, born in Chinle, was raised on the state's Navajo reservation, where his artistic abilities became evident at an early age. Today, Gorman's sculptures, drawings, and paintings are recognized for their expressive, finely wrought treatment of traditional Native American subjects. The creations of Gorman and other Arizona artists are displayed in such cultural institutions as the Phoenix Art Museum; the Museum of Northern Arizona, in Flagstaff; the Arizona State Museum, in Tucson; the sprawling Navajo Museum, Library, and Visitor Center on the Navajo Indian Reservation in northeastern Arizona; and at the many art shows held on the grounds of Prescott's Courthouse Plaza.

▲ Navajo craftspeople are world famous for their handwoven textiles *(top)* and pottery *(inset)*.

Literature

Ohio-born novelist Zane Grey (1872–1939), whose works include *The Last of the Plainsmen* (1908) and *Riders of the Purple Sage* (1912), set many of his novels in the Colorado Plateau region of Utah and Arizona. Grey almost single-handedly invented the genre of the Western novel. Contemporary best-selling author Tony Hillerman writes mysteries chronicling the adventures of Jim Chee, a Navajo man who leads a double life as a police officer and tribal shaman-in-training. Pennsylvania-born novelist and essayist Edward Abbey (1927–1989), author of *The Monkey Wrench Gang*, was associated with the Arizona desert for much of his distinguished writing career. Abbey is best remembered for his powerfully descriptive writing, both in fiction and nonfiction, as well as for his devotion to Arizona environmental causes. Although he did not live in Arizona himself, cartoonist George Herriman set his most famous cartoon, "Krazy Kat," in Coconino County. Herriman visited the state and was captivated by the scenery. He used the strangely shaped buttes and mesas that he saw there for the backdrop to the zany adventures of Krazy Kat, Ignatz Mouse, and Offisa Pup.

Sports and Recreation

Phoenix is home to professional basketball, baseball, football, and hockey franchises. The Phoenix Suns have been playing basketball in Phoenix since 1968 and have had twelve seasons of fifty or more wins. They won the division championship in 1981. The Phoenix Mercury, a Women's National Basketball Association (WNBA) team, began playing in 1997.

A World Unto Itself

Biosphere II *(below)* is a greenhouse-like dome located near Tucson. The idea was to create an environment with the minimum elements necessary to sustain life. A team of scientists lived inside the dome from 1991 to 1993, in order to determine whether human beings could survive within such a closed environment. The experiment was important for other ventures, including a possible months-long flight to Mars, which would place similar demands on astronauts.

The scientific value of Biosphere II was questioned, however, because the scientists pumped pure oxygen into the dome and used purification equipment to scrub carbon dioxide from the air. In 1993–1994 a second crew was sealed in the dome for six months. Although of shorter duration than its predecessor, this experiment was more scientifically successful.

The Arizona Diamondbacks began playing baseball in Phoenix in 1998 and won their first World Series in 2001, beating the New York Yankees behind the pitching of Arizona local Curt Schilling and his teammate Randy Johnson (both men shared the Most Valuable Player award for the series). Arizona shares with Florida the distinction of being a spring training base for Major League Baseball, serving such teams as the Chicago Cubs and the Seattle Mariners. Spring training is a major tourist draw for the state.

The Arizona Cardinals are the longest, continuously playing professional football franchise in the nation. Founded in 1898, the franchise has played in several cities under different names. After twenty-eight years in St. Louis, the Cardinals moved to Arizona in 1988. The team plays in the Arizona State University stadium in Tempe and is currently the only professional football team to play on a college field.

The Phoenix Coyotes, Arizona's National Hockey League (NHL) team, are owned by hockey legend Wayne Gretzky. They were once the Winnipeg Jets. Motor sports are also popular in Arizona. The Phoenix International Raceway, known as "the world's fastest oval," hosts frequent Indy car races as well as stock car events.

Scottsdale is a favorite spot for golfers, with courses set amid the splendor of the desert. One of the world's top five golfers, Phil Mickelson, played Arizona's links as a student at Arizona State University. The state also draws hikers and rock climbers from all around the world. On the Colorado River, both fishing and white-water rafting are popular. Lake Havasu attracts both boaters and swimmers with its 450 miles (724 km) of sunny shoreline.

▲ Diamondback Damian Miller hits a grand slam home run in Phoenix, April 2, 2002.

Sport	Team	Home
Baseball	Arizona Diamondbacks	Bank One Ballpark, Phoenix
Basketball	Phoenix Suns	America West Arena, Phoenix
Womens Basketball	Phoenix Mercury	America West Arena, Phoenix
Football	Arizona Cardinals	Arizona State University Stadium, Tempe
Hockey	Phoenix Coyotes	America West Arena, Phoenix

DID YOU KNOW?

The Arizona Diamondbacks are not the only connection the Grand Canyon State has to Major League Baseball. The Seattle Mariners and the San Diego Padres conduct their spring training in Arizona's Peoria Sports Complex; the Chicago Cubs train in Mesa; the Anaheim Angels shape up in Tempe; the San Francisco Giants warm up in Scottsdale; and the Milwaukee Brewers train in Maryvale. Tucson is a training base for both the Chicago White Sox and the Colorado Rockies, while Phoenix hosts the Oakland As.

Libraries and Museums

Arizona supports a wealth of public libraries and museums. The two largest libraries are part of the state's two major universities, Arizona State University and the University of Arizona. By some accounts, the territory's first library was opened in the 1860s by famed pistol manufacturer Samuel Colt, who wanted to establish a lending library for his mine workers in Arivaca. During the 1870s, Tucson established a rental library, not unlike a modern video store. The Arizona Territorial Library opened in 1864, and it later became the Department of Library, Archives, and Public Records. By 1878, the cities of Phoenix and Prescott had their own small public libraries, which have since evolved into large, metropolitan library systems.

Modern Arizona abounds with specialized museums dedicated to a wide variety of subjects, ranging from science to art to history to Native American cultures. Among the oldest of these are the Arizona Historical Society's museum and the Arizona State Museum, both in Tucson. The Tucson area is also the location of the International Wildlife Museum, the Pima Air and Space Museum, and the Arizona-Sonora Desert Museum, which is one of the state's great outdoor attractions. The Center for Creative Photography, located at the University of Arizona in Tucson, is home to a priceless collection of photographs by Ansel Adams, the famed twentieth-century U.S. photographer.

Phoenix is home to the Heard Museum, which focuses on Native American artwork; Pueblo Grande Museum, which displays the remains of a prehistoric Native village; the Arizona State Capitol Museum, which preserves and chronicles state government history; and the Phoenix Art Museum. Mesa offers the Champlin Fighter Museum, where fighter aircraft from numerous wars can be seen close-up. Visitors to Flagstaff can see Native American arts and crafts at the Museum of Northern Arizona.

▼ Kitt Peak National Observatory on the Tohono O'odham Indian Reservation has more optical telescopes than any other observatory in the world.

Historical and Cultural Sites

Arizona's Native American heritage can be explored at many places in the state. The Apache Trail in Tonto National Forest is a scenic mountain highway that provides access to fascinating ruins left behind by ancient Native American civilizations. The Navajo settlement of Oraibi has been in existence for more than eight centuries, making it one of North America's oldest, continuously inhabited places. Other notable Arizona cultural institutions include the ruins of Native American cliff dwellings at Montezuma Castle National Monument near Camp Verde.

The Grady Gammage Memorial Auditorium, at Arizona State University in Tempe, was architect Frank Lloyd Wright's last major building. Wright's winter home, Taliesin West, still stands in Scottsdale. At Prescott's Sharlot Hall Museum, period buildings, including the first governor's mansion, are on display. Established in 1700 by Father Eusebio Kino, San Xavier del Bac is perhaps the best maintained of Arizona's early Spanish missions. Located near Tucson, it is both an active church and a historical preserve, displaying collections of carvings and paintings of extraordinary beauty. Fremont House, in Tucson, preserves nineteenth-century furniture and decor. The 125-acre (50-ha) Phoenix Zoo, established in 1962 by philanthropist Robert E. Maytag, is home to approximately 1,400 animals, which live in habitats ranging from African savannas to tropical rain forests.

▲ The ruins of a cliff-dwelling society can be seen at Montezuma Castle National Monument in Camp Verde.

A Matter of Character

We judge individual men and women as we do nations
and races — by the character of their achievement
and by their achievement of character.

— *Edward Abbey, author, 1927-1988*

Following are only a few of the thousands of people who were born, died, or spent much of their lives
in Arizona and made extraordinary contributions to the state and the nation.

COCHISE

APACHE LEADER

BORN: *circa 1815, Chiricahua Territory, northern Mexico*
DIED: *June 8, 1874, new Chiricahua Reservation*

Although the Chiricahua Apache
chief Cochise (which means "firewood")
maintained peaceful relations with
southeastern Arizona's Anglo settlers,
a deadly mistake by Lieutenant George
Bascom of the Union Army, in 1861,
changed that forever. Cochise
stood falsely accused of having
kidnapped a local child. In
an effort to secure the child's
release, Bascom captured
the chief and several
members of his family.
After Cochise escaped,
Bascom hanged his
remaining prisoners.
Cochise and his people
were later proved innocent,
but the damage had been done. Cochise
and his followers spent the next decade
raiding isolated ranches, mining posts,
and stagecoaches, until U.S. troops
and frontiersman Thomas J. Jeffords
negotiated their surrender — and their
move to a reservation — in 1872.

GERONIMO

APACHE LEADER

BORN: *circa 1829, near Clifton*
DIED: *February 17, 1909, Fort Sill, OK*

Bedonkohe Chiricahua Apache
warrior Goyathlay (Geronimo)
is famous for leading raids
against Mexican and U.S.
soldiers. Geronimo (*left*)
swore vengeance against the
Mexicans, whom he blamed
for the ambush that killed
his family in 1858.
Geronimo's battle prowess

soon became legendary, prompting many Mexicans to assert that he possessed supernatural powers. The United States government began pursuing Geronimo and his brother-in-law, Juh, in 1875 because of their raids on Anglo settlements in eastern Arizona. After years of guerrilla warfare, Geronimo surrendered to General Nelson Miles on September 4, 1886 — making him the last of the Apache war chiefs to be captured. Geronimo was imprisoned in Florida and then moved in 1894 to Fort Sill, in Oklahoma. Geronimo's dictated memoirs were published as *Geronimo's Story of His Life* in 1906.

GEORGE CROOK
MILITARY LEADER

BORN: *September 8, 1830, near Dayton, OH*
DIED: *March 21, 1890, Chicago, IL*

Major General George Crook (*right*) led U.S. Army forces in campaigns against the Apache in the American Southwest. Known for his fair and careful dealings with Native people, Crook helped settle Native American uprisings in Arizona and Idaho, and he later became a crucial decision-maker in the 1876 Sioux War. In 1882 Crook pursued Apache warriors, led by Geronimo, from Arizona into Mexico, and by 1883 he had persuaded most of Geronimo's people to remain peaceably on reservation land. After Geronimo and several of his warriors escaped from reservation custody, Crook received harsh criticism for his leniency. During his final years, Crook spoke out against U.S. incursions against the Native Americans and wrote his memoirs. The Lakota chief Red Cloud said that Crook "never lied to us," and that he "gave the people hope."

PERCIVAL LOWELL
ASTRONOMER

BORN: *March 13, 1855, Boston, MA*
DIED: *November 12, 1916, Flagstaff*

Percival Lowell was a globe-trotting diplomat, international businessman, author, and mathematician. In 1894, he established an astronomical observatory (the Lowell Observatory) near Flagstaff, on a site he dubbed Mars Hill because of his intense interest in the Red Planet. Prior to founding his observatory, Lowell had been obsessed with the writings of the Italian astronomer Giovanni Schiaparelli, whose reports of the existence of Martian canali ("channels") led to Lowell's mistaken belief that Mars was inhabited by intelligent canal builders. Despite this belief, which was proved false by the *Mariner* probes of the 1960s, the Lowell Observatory has contributed greatly to the advancement of astronomy. Lowell's 1902 assertion that an unseen planet (Pluto) would be found orbiting beyond Neptune was confirmed fourteen years after his death.

FRANK LLOYD WRIGHT
ARCHITECT

BORN: *June 8, 1867, Richland Center, WI*
DIED: *April 9, 1959, Phoenix*

Frank Lloyd Wright was a major figure in modern architecture. Through his innovative designs and his writings,

Wright (*right*) defined a new architectural style that was based upon forms found in nature — an approach he called "organic architecture." Educated in civil engineering at the University of Wisconsin, Wright later relocated near Chicago, where his genius for architectural design flourished. Wright's houses were distinctive for their asymmetry, horizontality, low rooflines, and numerous skylights. Among Wright's most spectacular buildings have been the Guggenheim Museum in New York City, the Imperial Hotel in Tokyo, and his winter home, called Taliesin West. Wright used this famous house, located in Scottsdale, as part of a campus for training his architectural disciples. Taliesin West remains a major Arizona tourist destination.

LOUIS TEWANIMA
ATHLETE
BORN: *circa 1879, Shongopovi, Hopi Reservation*
DIED: *January 19, 1969, near Shongopovi*

Louis Tewanima, a Hopi and an alumnus of Pennsylvania's Carlisle Indian School, was one of the greatest long-distance runners in U.S. history. Tewanima first distinguished himself by winning the silver medal in the 1912 Olympic Games in Stockholm, Sweden. For fifty-two years, the record Tewanima set in the 10,000-meter race was unbroken in the United States. Notable for his graceful running style, Tewanima was included as a member of the All-Time U.S. Olympic Track and Field Team. In 1957, Tewanima was honored as the first inductee into the Arizona Sports Hall of Fame.

BARRY GOLDWATER
POLITICIAN
BORN: *January 1, 1909, Phoenix*
DIED: *May 29, 1998, Pleasant Valley*

The son of a prosperous Phoenix merchant, Republican Barry Morris Goldwater became a U.S. senator representing Arizona in 1952. Goldwater was a hard-line conservative who spoke out against big government and favored returning more power to state and local authorities. He vigorously opposed communism, friendship with the Soviet Union, and federal welfare programs, while championing the U.S. war effort in Vietnam and the privatization of public utilities. Goldwater made an unsuccessful bid for the White House in the 1964 presidential election, losing to the incumbent president, Lyndon B. Johnson. Goldwater remained a member of the U.S. Senate until his retirement in 1987.

CHARLES MINGUS
MUSICIAN
BORN: *April 22, 1922, Nogales*
DIED: *January 5, 1979, Cuernavaca, Mexico*

Charles Mingus was a master of the string bass and the piano, and his compositions were critical in shaping modern jazz music. Mingus began experimenting with unusual sounds in the 1950s. These innovations quickly placed him in the forefront of modern jazz composers. His virtuosity on the string bass helped establish the instrument as a bona fide solo instrument. One of Mingus's admirers was the pop singer and composer Joni Mitchell, with whom he recorded in 1978. Mingus composed "Epitaph," a suite for jazz orchestra, which was not performed publicly until eleven years after his death. *The New Yorker* magazine hailed "Epitaph" as the first advance in jazz composition since Duke Ellington's "Black, Brown, and Beige" (1943).

MARTY ROBBINS
COUNTRY SINGER
BORN: *September 26, 1925, Glendale*
DIED: *December 8, 1982, Nashville, TN*

One of nine children, Marty Robbins was a versatile country-and-western singer, composer, and guitarist. During his career, he recorded almost seventy albums and topped the country singles chart no fewer than eighteen times. Robbins hosted his own television show, "Country Caravan," broadcast from Phoenix during the late 1940s, and he became a fixture on the *Grand Ole Opry* by 1953. Among Robbins's best-remembered hits are "I Couldn't Keep from Crying" (1953), "I'll Go on Alone" (1953), "A White Sport Coat and a Pink Carnation" (1957), and "El Paso" (1959), the last of which won the first Grammy Award for best country song.

CÉSAR CHAVEZ
LABOR ORGANIZER
BORN: *March 31, 1927, Yuma*
DIED: *April 23, 1993, San Luis*

Senator Robert F. Kennedy once called César Estrada Chavez "one of the heroic figures of our time." The son of a migrant farm worker, Chavez founded the United Farm Workers (UFW), focusing public attention on

the miserable pay and often horrible working conditions of America's agricultural laborers. During most of the 1950s, Chavez worked on behalf of the Community Service Organization, a progressive political group that helped the poor and disadvantaged register to vote. Chavez pressured California's farmers to sign labor contracts with the UFW by initiating a series of highly effective national boycotts of grapes, wine, and lettuce, and by going on well-publicized hunger strikes. Like Martin Luther King, Jr., Chavez was an advocate and practitioner of nonviolent protest. In 1994, President Bill Clinton posthumously awarded Chavez the Presidential Medal of Freedom.

SANDRA DAY O'CONNOR
SUPREME COURT JUSTICE
BORN: *March 26, 1930, El Paso, TX*

Born in El Paso, Texas, in 1930, Sandra Day O'Connor was raised on an Arizona cattle ranch. She became the first woman to serve on the U.S. Supreme Court. She is known as a moderate conservative. O'Connor graduated from Stanford University and settled in Phoenix in 1952. She worked as a lawyer, an assistant attorney general, a state senator, and a judge in Arizona. In July 1981, President Ronald Reagan chose her as his first appointee to the U.S. Supreme Court, and, after her confirmation by the U.S. Senate, she was sworn in as an associate justice on September 25, 1981.

Arizona
History At-A-Glance

1539
While seeking the gold of the mythical Seven Cities of Cibola, Spanish priest Fray Marcos de Niza becomes the first European to survey Arizona.

1752
The Tubac presidio becomes the first European settlement in Arizona.

1824
Arizona is incorporated into Mexico, after Mexico secures independence from Spain.

1854
With the Gadsden Purchase, the United States adds formerly Mexican territory to southern Arizona.

1862
Confederate troops seize Tucson.

1863
The U.S. Congress establishes the Arizona Territory, separating Arizona from New Mexico.

1864
Kit Carson captures more than eight thousand Navajo and forces them out of Arizona.

1871
Arizona opens its first public school in Tucson.

1877
The Southern Pacific Railroad comes to Arizona; large silver deposits are discovered at Tombstone.

1881
The Earp brothers and Doc Holliday take on the Ike Clanton gang in the famous gunfight at the O.K. Corral, in Tombstone.

1885
The Territorial Normal School (later Arizona State University) is established at Tempe; the University of Arizona opens at Tucson.

1886
Geronimo and his Apache warriors surrender to U.S. forces. Geronimo is subsequently exiled from Arizona.

1600   **1700**   **1800**

1492
Christopher Columbus comes to New World.

1607
Capt. John Smith and three ships land on Virginia coast and start first English settlement in New World — Jamestown.

1754–63
French and Indian War.

1773
Boston Tea Party.

1776
Declaration of Independence adopted July 4.

1777
Articles of Confederation adopted by Continental Congress.

1787
U.S. Constitution written.

1812–14
War of 1812.

United States
History At-A-Glance

▼ This 1908 photograph shows a petrified bridge in the Petrified Forest.

1936
Construction ends on the Hoover Dam, creating a large artificial lake (Lake Mead) behind it.

1965
Lorna Lockwood becomes the first woman chief justice of a state supreme court.

1969
Navajo Community College is opened in Tsaile, the first college established on a Native-American reservation.

1981
Sandra Day O'Connor becomes the first female member of the U.S. Supreme Court.

1997
Governor Fife Symington III resigns after being convicted on seven counts of financial fraud.

1889
Phoenix becomes the capital of the Arizona Territory.

1912
Arizona enters the Union as the nation's forty-eighth state.

1948
The U.S. and Arizona Supreme Courts grant voting rights to Native Americans.

1968
The U.S. Congress authorizes the Central Arizona Project, which will deliver water to Tucson, Phoenix, and other areas.

1975
Raul H. Castro takes office as the first Mexican-American governor of Arizona.

1988
Governor Evan Mecham is forced from office. Rose Mofford replaces him, becoming Arizona's first female governor.

1998
Women are elected to the offices of governor, secretary of state, attorney general, treasurer, and superintendent of public instruction.

1800 | **1900** | **2000**

1848
Gold discovered in California draws eighty thousand prospectors in the 1849 Gold Rush.

1861–65
Civil War.

1869
Transcontinental railroad completed.

1917–18
U.S. involvement in World War I.

1929
Stock market crash ushers in Great Depression.

1941–45
U.S. involvement in World War II.

1950–53
U.S. fights in the Korean War.

1964–73
U.S. involvement in Vietnam War.

2000
George W. Bush wins the closest presidential election in history.

2001
A terrorist attack in which four hijacked airliners crash into New York City's World Trade Center, the Pentagon, and farmland in western Pennsylvania leaves thousands dead or injured.

Festivals and Fun for All

Check web site for exact date and directions.

American Indian Exposition, Tucson

This annual event draws together performers and artists for competition and display from the many Native American nations of the United States.
www.usaindianinfo.org/expo.htm

Arizona National Stock Show, Phoenix

Arizona's largest livestock show begins in late December and runs into early January. Attractions include exhibits from twenty-seven states and Canada, one of Arizona's largest high school rodeos, professional rodeo and cowboy demonstrations, and the Cowboy Classics Western Art and Gear Show.
www.anls.org

Arizona's Own Garlic Festival, Sedona

In late June, Arizona's Own Garlic Festival celebrates the "stinking rose" — garlic — at the Poco Diablo Resort. The event features cooking demonstrations, children's activities, arts and crafts booths — and breath mints.
www.americanjourneys.com/AZ-Sedona/events.html

Arizona State Fair, Phoenix

Held for two weeks during late October and early November, the fair is the largest annual event of its kind in the state. Rodeo spectator events, livestock shows, and live performances by some of the biggest names in music are only a few of the attractions.
www.azstatefair.com

Easter Sunrise Service, Grand Canyon

Easter weekend brings multitudes of visitors to the Shrine of the Ages, located at Mather Point on the Grand Canyon's scenic South Rim. This Easter observance is the Grand Canyon's largest single annual event, attracting people from all over the world.
www.infomagic.net /~gccc/ EASTER %20SERVICE.html

Festival of the Arts, Tempe

Each March and December, the Mill Avenue Merchants Association produces the Spring and Fall Festival of the Arts. More than four hundred of the nation's finest artisans display sculptures, wooden toys, handwoven bags, oil paintings, pottery, and food. Other attractions include live entertainment and activities for all ages.
www.tempe.gov/newsrel/eachyear.htm

Frontier Days, Prescott

During the first week of July, the world's oldest rodeo comes to Prescott, the birthplace of the sport. The festival features a parade, dancing, and fireworks, as well as traditional rodeo.
www.worldsoldestrodeo.com

Glendale Chocolate Affaire, Glendale

In early February, Glendale celebrates chocolate and romance with a gathering of local and national chocolatiers, featuring a gourmet marketplace, fine arts, and carriage rides.
tour.glendaleaz.com/chocolateaffaire.html

▲ Good times at the Tucson Harvest Festival.

La Fiesta de los Vaqueros Rodeo, Tucson

Held during the third week of February, this cowboy celebration numbers among North America's top fifteen professional rodeos and is enshrined in the Pro Rodeo Hall of Fame.
www.tucsonrodeo.com

London Bridge Days,
Lake Havasu City

In mid-October, Lake Havasu City honors the London Bridge with commemorative events held in a variety of locations in this scenic resort town.
www.coloradoriverinfo.com/events
/havasu.city.shtml

Navajo Nation Fair,
Window Rock

This celebration of Navajo culture convenes in early September, featuring arts and crafts, cultural exhibits, a beautiful baby contest, song and dance demonstrations, a fried bread contest, and a carnival.
www.navajonationfair.com

Old-Time Fiddlers Contest, Payson

At the end of September, Payson attracts the region's finest fiddlers, ages six through eighty-six, for a country and bluegrass musical competition. This two-day event also features noontime 21-fiddle salutes, cowboy poets, storytellers, Irish step-dancers, a children's music workshop, fiddle makers, and leather workers.
www.carizona.com/rim/events.html

Sedona Jazz on the Rocks, Sedona

September brings four days of jazz and blues to a variety of musical venues in the desert town of Sedona.
www.sedonajazz.com

Tucson Harvest Festival, Tucson

During the first weekend in November, the Tucson Convention Center is transformed into a magical marketplace of handmade crafts, homemade foods, and spirited entertainment.
www.harvestfestival.com

Wyatt Earp Days,
Tombstone

May brings a celebration of the wild and woolly history of the frontier boomtown of Tombstone, best known as the site of the legendary gunfight at the O.K. Corral.
www.tombstone.org

Books

Anderson, Joan. *Batboy: An Inside Look at Spring Training*. New York: Lodestar, 1996. Experience spring training in Scottsdale through the eyes of a thirteen-year-old batboy.

Anderson, Peter. *A Grand Canyon Journey: Tracing Time in Stone*. New York: Franklin Watts, 1997. Readers can take an imaginary tour through the Grand Canyon, learning about its ecology, history, and wildlife along the way.

Schwarz, Melissa. *Cochise: Apache Chief*. Minneapolis, MN: Econo-Clad Books, 1999. The life story of the legendary Apache warrior, for younger readers.

Weir, Bill. *National Geographic Traveler: Arizona*. Washington, D.C.: National Geographic Society, 2001. A colorful and information-packed guide to Arizona's history, people, and attractions, written for a general audience of all ages.

Zannos, Susan. *César Chavez: A Real-Life Reader Biography*. Bear, DE: Mitchell Lane Publishers, Inc., 1998. César Chavez was involved in a lifelong struggle to secure the rights of migrant farm workers. His inspirational story is told here.

Web Sites

▶ Arizona's official state web site
www.az.gov/webapp/portal/

▶ Official web site of the state capital
www.ci.phoenix.az.us/

▶ Official web site of the Arizona Historical Society, Southern Arizona Division
w3.arizona.edu/~azhist/

▶ Kids Page
A web page sponsored by the office of Arizona's governor
www.governor.state.az.us/kids/kids.cfm

▶ Web site of the Grand Canyon Association
www.grandcanyon.org

Note: Page numbers in *italics* refer to illustrations, maps, or photographs.